The Crazy

The Bean Eaters

GWENDOLYN BROOKS

Harper & Brothers, Publishers New York

THE BEAN EATERS

Printed in the United States of America

FIRST EDITION

C-K

Some of these poems were first published in HARPER'S MAGAZINE, POETRY, and VOICES.

In Honor of David Anderson Brooks, My Father

JULY 30, 1883–NOVEMBER 21, 1959

A dryness is upon the house
My father loved and tended.
Beyond his firm and sculptured door
His light and lease have ended.

He walks the valleys, now—replies
To sun and wind forever.
No more the cramping chamber's chill,
No more the hindering fever.

Now out upon the wide clean air
My father's soul revives,
All innocent of self-interest
And the fear that strikes and strives.

He who was Goodness, Gentleness,
And Dignity is free,
Translates to public Love
Old private charity.

CONTENTS

The Bean Eaters

The Explorer

Somehow to find a still spot in the noise
Was the frayed inner want, the winding, the frayed hope
Whose tatters he kept hunting through the din.
A satin peace somewhere.
A room of wily hush somewhere within.

So tipping down the scrambled halls he set
Vague hands on throbbing knobs. There were behind
Only spiraling, high human voices,
The scream of nervous affairs,
Wee griefs,
Grand griefs. And choices.

He feared most of all the choices, that cried to be taken.

There were no bourns.
There were no quiet rooms.

My Little 'Bout-town Gal

ROGER OF RHODES

My little 'bout-town gal has gone
'Bout town with powder and blue dye
On her pale lids and on her lips
Dye sits quite carminely.

I'm scarcely healthy-hearted or human.
What can I teach my cheated Woman?

My Tondeleyo, my black blonde
Will not be homing soon.
None shall secure her save the late the
Detective fingers of the moon.

Strong Men, Riding Horses

LESTER AFTER THE WESTERN

Strong Men, riding horses. In the West
On a range five hundred miles. A Thousand. Reaching
From dawn to sunset. Rested blue to orange.
From hope to crying. Except that Strong Men are
Desert-eyed. Except that Strong Men are
Pasted to stars already. Have their cars
Beneath them. Rentless, too. Too broad of chest
To shrink when the Rough Man hails. Too flailing
To redirect the Challenger, when the challenge
Nicks; slams; buttonholes. Too saddled.

I am not like that. I pay rent, am addled
By illegible landlords, run, if robbers call.

What mannerisms I present, employ,
Are camouflage, and what my mouths remark
To word-wall off that broadness of the dark
Is pitiful.
I am not brave at all.

The Bean Eaters

They eat beans mostly, this old yellow pair.
Dinner is a casual affair.
Plain chipware on a plain and creaking wood,
Tin flatware.

Two who are Mostly Good.
Two who have lived their day,
But keep on putting on their clothes
And putting things away.

And remembering . . .
Remembering, with twinklings and twinges,
As they lean over the beans in their rented back room that
is full of beads and receipts and dolls and cloths,
tobacco crumbs, vases and fringes.

We Real Cool

THE POOL PLAYERS.
SEVEN AT THE GOLDEN SHOVEL.

We real cool. We
Left school. We

Lurk late. We
Strike straight. We

Sing sin. We
Thin gin. We

Jazz June. We
Die soon.

Old Mary

My last defense
Is the present tense.

It little hurts me now to know
I shall not go

Cathedral-hunting in Spain
Nor cherrying in Michigan or Maine.

A Bronzeville Mother Loiters in Mississippi. Meanwhile, a Mississippi Mother Burns Bacon

From the first it had been like a
Ballad. It had the beat inevitable. It had the blood.
A wildness cut up, and tied in little bunches,
Like the four-line stanzas of the ballads she had never quite
Understood — the ballads they had set her to, in school.

Herself: the milk-white maid, the "maid mild"
Of the ballad. Pursued
By the Dark Villain. Rescued by the Fine Prince.
The Happiness-Ever-After.
That was worth anything.
It was good to be a "maid mild."
That made the breath go fast.

Her bacon burned. She
Hastened to hide it in the step-on can, and
Drew more strips from the meat case. The eggs and sour-
milk biscuits

Did well. She set out a jar
Of her new quince preserve.

. . . But there was a something about the matter of the Dark Villain.
He should have been older, perhaps.
The hacking down of a villain was more fun to think about
When his menace possessed undisputed breadth, undisputed height,
And a harsh kind of vice.
And best of all, when his history was cluttered
With the bones of many eaten knights and princesses.

The fun was disturbed, then all but nullified
When the Dark Villain was a blackish child
Of fourteen, with eyes still too young to be dirty,
And a mouth too young to have lost every reminder
Of its infant softness.

That boy must have been surprised! For
These were grown-ups. Grown-ups were supposed to be wise.
And the Fine Prince — and that other — so tall, so broad, so
Grown! Perhaps the boy had never guessed
That the trouble with grown-ups was that under the magnificent shell of adulthood, just under,
Waited the baby full of tantrums.

It occurred to her that there may have been something
Ridiculous in the picture of the Fine Prince
Rushing (rich with the breadth and height and
Mature solidness whose lack, in the Dark Villain, was impressing her,
Confronting her more and more as this first day after the trial
And acquittal wore on) rushing
With his heavy companion to hack down (unhorsed)
That little foe.
So much had happened, she could not remember now what that foe had done
Against her, or if anything had been done.
The one thing in the world that she did know and knew
With terrifying clarity was that her composition
Had disintegrated. That, although the pattern prevailed,
The breaks were everywhere. That she could think
Of no thread capable of the necessary
Sew-work.

She made the babies sit in their places at the table.
Then, before calling Him, she hurried
To the mirror with her comb and lipstick. It was necessary
To be more beautiful than ever.
The beautiful wife.
For sometimes she fancied he looked at her as though
Measuring her. As if he considered, Had she been worth It?

Had *she* been worth the blood, the cramped cries, the little stuttering bravado,
The gradual dulling of those Negro eyes,
The sudden, overwhelming *little-boyness* in that barn?
Whatever she might feel or half-feel, the lipstick necessity was something apart. He must never conclude
That she had not been worth It.

He sat down, the Fine Prince, and
Began buttering a biscuit. He looked at his hands.
He twisted in his chair, he scratched his nose.
He glanced again, almost secretly, at his hands.
More papers were in from the North, he mumbled. More meddling headlines.
With their pepper-words, "bestiality," and "barbarism," and
"Shocking."
The half-sneers he had mastered for the trial worked across
His sweet and pretty face.

What he'd like to do, he explained, was kill them all.
The time lost. The unwanted fame.
Still, it had been fun to show those intruders
A thing or two. To show that snappy-eyed mother,
That sassy, Northern, brown-black ——

Nothing could stop Mississippi.

He knew that. Big Fella
Knew that.
And, what was so good, Mississippi knew that.
Nothing and nothing could stop Mississippi.
They could send in their petitions, and scar
Their newspapers with bleeding headlines. Their governors
Could appeal to Washington. . . .

"What I want," the older baby said, "is 'lasses on my
  jam."
Whereupon the younger baby
Picked up the molasses pitcher and threw
The molasses in his brother's face. Instantly
The Fine Prince leaned across the table and slapped
The small and smiling criminal.

She did not speak. When the Hand
Came down and away, and she could look at her child,
At her baby-child,
She could think only of blood.
Surely her baby's cheek
Had disappeared, and in its place, surely,
Hung a heaviness, a lengthening red, a red that had no end.
She shook her head. It was not true, of course.
It was not true at all. The
Child's face was as always, the
Color of the paste in her paste-jar.

She left the table, to the tune of the children's lamentations, which were shriller
Than ever. She
Looked out of a window. She said not a word. *That*
Was one of the new Somethings —
The fear,
Tying her as with iron.

Suddenly she felt his hands upon her. He had followed her
To the window. The children were whimpering now.
Such bits of tots. And she, their mother,
Could not protect them. She looked at her shoulders, still
Gripped in the claim of his hands. She tried, but could not resist the idea
That a red ooze was seeping, spreading darkly, thickly, slowly,
Over her white shoulders, her own shoulders,
And over all of Earth and Mars.

He whispered something to her, did the Fine Prince, something
About love, something about love and night and intention.

She heard no hoof-beat of the horse and saw no flash of the shining steel.

He pulled her face around to meet
His, and there it was, close close,

For the first time in all those days and nights.
His mouth, wet and red,
So very, very, very red,
Closed over hers.

Then a sickness heaved within her. The courtroom Coca-Cola,
The courtroom beer and hate and sweat and drone,
Pushed like a wall against her. She wanted to bear it.
But his mouth would not go away and neither would the
Decapitated exclamation points in that Other Woman's eyes.

She did not scream.
She stood there.
But a hatred for him burst into glorious flower,
And its perfume enclasped them—big,
Bigger than all magnolias.

The last bleak news of the ballad.
The rest of the rugged music.
The last quatrain.

The Last Quatrain of the Ballad of Emmett Till

AFTER THE MURDER,
AFTER THE BURIAL

Emmett's mother is a pretty-faced thing;
the tint of pulled taffy.
She sits in a red room,
drinking black coffee.
She kisses her killed boy.
And she is sorry.
Chaos in windy grays
through a red prairie.

Mrs. Small

Mrs. Small went to the kitchen for her pocketbook
And came back to the living room with a peculiar look
And the coffee pot.
Pocketbook. Pot.
Pot. Pocketbook.

The insurance man was waiting there
With superb and cared-for hair.
His face did not have much time.
He did not glance with sublime
Love upon the little plump tan woman
With the half-open mouth and the half-mad eyes
And the smile half-human
Who stood in the middle of the living-room floor planning
  apple pies
And graciously offering him a steaming coffee pot.
Pocketbook. Pot.

"Oh!" Mrs. Small came to her senses,
Peered earnestly through thick lenses,

Jumped terribly. This, too, was a mistake,
Unforgivable no matter how much she had to bake.
For there can be no whiter whiteness than this one:
An insurance man's shirt on its morning run.
This Mrs. Small now soiled
With a pair of brown
Spurts (just recently boiled)
Of the "very best coffee in town."

"The best coffee in town is what *you* make, Delphine! There
is none dandier!"
Those were the words of the pleased Jim Small —
Who was no bandier of words at all.
Jim Small was likely to give you a good swat
When he was *not*
Pleased. He was, absolutely, no bandier.

"I don't know where my mind is this morning,"
Said Mrs. Small, scorning
Apologies! For there was so much
For which to apologize! Oh such
Mountains of things, she'd never get anything done
If she begged forgiveness for each one.

She paid him.

But apologies and her hurry would not mix.
The six

Daughters were a-yell, a-scramble, in the hall. The four
Sons (horrors) could not be heard any more.

No.
The insurance man would have to glare
Idiotically into her own sterile stare
A moment — then depart,
Leaving her to release her heart
And dizziness
And silence her six
And mix
Her spices and core
And slice her apples, and find her four.
Continuing her part
Of the world's business.

Jessie Mitchell's Mother

Into her mother's bedroom to wash the ballooning body.
"My mother is jelly-hearted and she has a brain of jelly:
Sweet, quiver-soft, irrelevant. Not essential.
Only a habit would cry if she should die.
A pleasant sort of fool without the least iron. . . .
Are you better, mother, do you think it will come today?"
The stretched yellow rag that was Jessie Mitchell's mother
Reviewed her. Young, and so thin, and so straight.
So straight! as if nothing could ever bend her.
But poor men would bend her, and doing things with poor men,
Being much in bed, and babies would bend her over,
And the rest of things in life that were for poor women,
Coming to them grinning and pretty with intent to bend and to kill.
Comparisons shattered her heart, ate at her bulwarks:
The shabby and the bright: she, almost hating her daughter,
Crept into an old sly refuge: "Jessie's black
And her way will be black, and jerkier even than mine.

Mine, in fact, because I was lovely, had flowers
Tucked in the jerks, flowers were here and there. . . ."
She revived for the moment settled and dried-up triumphs,
Forced perfume into old petals, pulled up the droop,
Refueled
Triumphant long-exhaled breaths.
Her exquisite yellow youth. . . .

The Chicago Defender *Sends a Man to Little Rock*

FALL, 1957

In Little Rock the people bear
Babes, and comb and part their hair
And watch the want ads, put repair
To roof and latch. While wheat toast burns
A woman waters multiferns.

Time upholds or overturns
The many, tight, and small concerns.

In Little Rock the people sing
Sunday hymns like anything,
Through Sunday pomp and polishing.

And after testament and tunes,
Some soften Sunday afternoons
With lemon tea and Lorna Doones.

I forecast

And I believe
Come Christmas Little Rock will cleave
To Christmas tree and trifle, weave,
From laugh and tinsel, texture fast.

In Little Rock is baseball; Barcarolle.
That hotness in July . . . the uniformed figures raw and
    implacable
And not intellectual,
Batting the hotness or clawing the suffering dust.
The Open Air Concert, on the special twilight green . . .
When Beethoven is brutal or whispers to lady-like air.
Blanket-sitters are solemn, as Johann troubles to lean
To tell them what to mean. . . .

There is love, too, in Little Rock. Soft women softly
Opening themselves in kindness,
Or, pitying one's blindness,
Awaiting one's pleasure
In azure
Glory with anguished rose at the root. . . .
To wash away old semi-discomfitures.
They re-teach purple and unsullen blue.
The wispy soils go. And uncertain
Half-havings have they clarified to sures.

In Little Rock they know
Not answering the telephone is a way of rejecting life,

That it is our business to be bothered, is our business
To cherish bores or boredom, be polite
To lies and love and many-faceted fuzziness.

I scratch my head, massage the hate-I-had.
I blink across my prim and pencilled pad.
The saga I was sent for is not down.
Because there is a puzzle in this town.
The biggest News I do not dare
Telegraph to the Editor's chair:
"They are like people everywhere."

The angry Editor would reply
In hundred harryings of Why.

And true, they are hurling spittle, rock,
Garbage and fruit in Little Rock.
And I saw coiling storm a-writhe
On bright madonnas. And a scythe
Of men harassing brownish girls.
(The bows and barrettes in the curls
And braids declined away from joy.)

I saw a bleeding brownish boy. . . .

The lariat lynch-wish I deplored.

The loveliest lynchee was our Lord.

The Lovers of the Poor

arrive. The Ladies from the Ladies' Betterment
League
Arrive in the afternoon, the late light slanting
In diluted gold bars across the boulevard brag
Of proud, seamed faces with mercy and murder hinting
Here, there, interrupting, all deep and debonair,
The pink paint on the innocence of fear;
Walk in a gingerly manner up the hall.
Cutting with knives served by their softest care,
Served by their love, so barbarously fair.
Whose mothers taught: You'd better not be cruel!
You had better not throw stones upon the wrens!
Herein they kiss and coddle and assault
Anew and dearly in the innocence
With which they baffle nature. Who are full,
Sleek, tender-clad, fit, fiftyish, a-glow, all
Sweetly abortive, hinting at fat fruit,
Judge it high time that fiftyish fingers felt
Beneath the lovelier planes of enterprise.
To resurrect. To moisten with milky chill.

To be a random hitching post or plush.
To be, for wet eyes, random and handy hem.
Their guild is giving money to the poor.
The worthy poor. The very very worthy
And beautiful poor. Perhaps just not too swarthy?
Perhaps just not too dirty nor too dim
Nor — passionate. In truth, what they could wish
Is — something less than derelict or dull.
Not staunch enough to stab, though, gaze for gaze!
God shield them sharply from the beggar-bold!
The noxious needy ones whose battle's bald
Nonetheless for being voiceless, hits one down.
But it's all so bad! and entirely too much for them.
The stench; the urine, cabbage, and dead beans,
Dead porridges of assorted dusty grains,
The old smoke, *heavy* diapers, and, they're told,
Something called chitterlings. The darkness. Drawn
Darkness, or dirty light. The soil that stirs.
The soil that looks the soil of centuries.
And for that matter the *general* oldness. Old
Wood. Old marble. Old tile. Old old old.
Not homekind Oldness! Not Lake Forest, Glencoe.
Nothing is sturdy, nothing is majestic,
There is no quiet drama, no rubbed glaze, no
Unkillable infirmity of such
A tasteful turn as lately they have left,
Glencoe, Lake Forest, and to which their cars
Must presently restore them. When they're done

With dullards and distortions of this fistic
Patience of the poor and put-upon.
        They've never seen such a make-do-ness as
Newspaper rugs before! In this, this "flat,"
Their hostess is gathering up the oozed, the rich
Rugs of the morning (tattered! the bespattered . . .),
Readies to spread clean rugs for afternoon.
Here is a scene for you. The Ladies look,
In horror, behind a substantial citizeness
Whose trains clank out across her swollen heart.
Who, arms akimbo, almost fills a door.
All tumbling children, quilts dragged to the floor
And tortured thereover, potato peelings, soft-
Eyed kitten, hunched-up, haggard, to-be-hurt.
        Their League is allotting largesse to the Lost.
But to put their clean, their pretty money, to put
Their money collected from delicate rose-fingers
Tipped with their hundred flawless rose-nails seems . . .
        They own Spode, Lowestoft, candelabra,
Mantels, and hostess gowns, and sunburst clocks,
Turtle soup, Chippendale, red satin "hangings,"
Aubussons and Hattie Carnegie. They Winter
In Palm Beach; cross the Water in June; attend,
When suitable, the nice Art Institute;
Buy the right books in the best bindings; saunter
On Michigan, Easter mornings, in sun or wind.
Oh Squalor! This sick four-story hulk, this fibre
With fissures everywhere! Why, what are bringings

Of loathe-love largesse? What shall peril hungers
So old old, what shall flatter the desolate?
Tin can, blocked fire escape and chitterling
And swaggering seeking youth and the puzzled wreckage
Of the middle passage, and urine and stale shames
And, again, the porridges of the underslung
And children children children. Heavens! That
Was a rat, surely, off there, in the shadows? Long
And long-tailed? Gray? The Ladies from the Ladies'
Betterment League agree it will be better
To achieve the outer air that rights and steadies,
To hie to a house that does not holler, to ring
Bells elsetime, better presently to cater
To no more Possibilities, to get
Away. Perhaps the money can be posted.
Perhaps they two may choose another Slum!
Some serious sooty half-unhappy home!—
Where loathe-love likelier may be invested.
　　　　Keeping their scented bodies in the center
Of the hall as they walk down the hysterical hall,
They allow their lovely skirts to graze no wall,
Are off at what they manage of a canter,
And, resuming all the clues of what they were,
Try to avoid inhaling the laden air.

A Sunset of the City

KATHLEEN EILEEN

Already I am no longer looked at with lechery or love.
My daughters and sons have put me away with marbles
and dolls,
Are gone from the house.
My husband and lovers are pleasant or somewhat polite
And night is night.

It is a real chill out,
The genuine thing.
I am not deceived, I do not think it is still summer
Because sun stays and birds continue to sing.

It is summer-gone that I see, it is summer-gone.
The sweet flowers indrying and dying down,
The grasses forgetting their blaze and consenting to
brown.

It is a real chill out. The fall crisp comes.

I am aware there is winter to heed.
There is no warm house
That is fitted with my need.

I am cold in this cold house this house
Whose washed echoes are tremulous down lost halls.
I am a woman, and dusty, standing among new affairs.
I am a woman who hurries through her prayers.

Tin intimations of a quiet core to be my
Desert and my dear relief
Come: there shall be such islanding from grief,
And small communion with the master shore.
Twang they. And I incline this ear to tin,
Consult a dual dilemma. Whether to dry
In humming pallor or to leap and die.

Somebody muffed it? Somebody wanted to joke.

A Man of the Middle Class

I'm what has gone out blithely and with noise
Returning! I'm what rushed around to pare
Down rind, to find fruit frozen under there.

I am bedraggled, with sundry dusts to be shed;
Trailing desperate tarnished tassels. These strident Aprils
With terrifying polkas and Bugle Calls
Confound me.

— Although I've risen! and my back is bold.
My tongue is brainy, choosing from among
Care, rage, surprise, despair, and choosing care.
I'm semi-splendid within what I've defended.

Yet, there I totter, there limp laxly. My
Uncomely trudge
To Plateau That and platitudinous Plateau
Whichever is no darling to my grudge-
Choked industry or usual alcohol.

I've roses to guard
In the architectural prettiness of my yard.
(But there are no paths remarkable for wide
Believable welcomes.)

I have loved directions.
I have loved orders and an iron to stride, I,
Whose hands are papers now,
Fit only for tossing in this outrageous air.

Not God nor grace nor candy balls
Will get me everything different and the same!

My wife has canvas walls.

My wife never quite forgets to put flowers in vases,
Bizarre prints in the most unusual places,
Give teas for poets, wear odoriferous furs.
An awful blooming is hers.

I've antique firearms. Blackamoors. Chinese
Rugs. Ivories.
Bronzes. Everything I Wanted.
But have I answers? Oh methinks
I've answers such as have
The executives I copied long ago,
The ones who, forfeiting Vicks salve,
Prayer book and Mother, shot themselves last Sunday.

All forsaking
All that was theirs but for their money's taking.
I've answers such as Giants used to know.
There's a Giant who'll jump next Monday; all forsaking
Wives, safes and solitaire
And the elegant statue standing at the foot of the stair.

Kid Bruin

ARRANGES ANOTHER TITLE DEFENSE

I rode into the golden yell
Of the hollow land of fame.
And when I mentioned rainbow
They did not know the name;

But thought it might have been there
And overnight have hied:
Adding that nothing in that land
Could be trapped or tied.
Trapped or tied or kissed for good
Or bound about the hand.

They could not swear to rainbow
In that hollow land.

The Ghost at the Quincy Club

All filmy down she drifts
In filmy stuffs and all.
Some gentle Gentile girl
Wafts down our Quincy hall.
This was a mansion once! —
With polished panels and all.

Where velvet voices lessened, stopped, and rose
Rise raucous Howdys. And a curse comes pure.
Yea it comes pure and challenges again
All ghost airs, graces, all daughters-of-gentlemen
Moth-soft, off-sweet. Demure.

Where Tea and Father were (each clear
And lemony) are dark folk, drinking beer.

The Crazy Woman

I shall not sing a May song.
A May song should be gay.
I'll wait until November
And sing a song of gray.

I'll wait until November.
That is the time for me.
I'll go out in the frosty dark
And sing most terribly.

And all the little people
Will stare at me and say,
"That is the Crazy Woman
Who would not sing in May."

Pete at the Zoo

I wonder if the elephant
Is lonely in his stall
When all the boys and girls are gone
And there's no shout at all,
And there's no one to stamp before,
No one to note his might.
Does he hunch up, as I do,
Against the dark of night?

Bronzeville Man with a Belt in the Back

In such an armor he may rise and raid
The dark cave after midnight, unafraid,
And slice the shadows with his able sword
Of good broad nonchalance, hashing them down.

And come out and accept the gasping crowd,
Shake off the praises with an airiness.
And, searching, see love shining in an eye,
But never smile.

In such an armor he cannot be slain.

A Lovely Love

LILLIAN'S

Let it be alleys. Let it be a hall
Whose janitor javelins epithet and thought
To cheapen hyacinth darkness that we sought
And played we found, rot, make the petals fall.
Let it be stairways, and a splintery box
Where you have thrown me, scraped me with your kiss,
Have honed me, have released me after this
Cavern kindness, smiled away our shocks.
That is the birthright of our lovely love
In swaddling clothes. Not like that Other one.
Not lit by any fondling star above.
Not found by any wise men, either. Run.
People are coming. They must not catch us here
Definitionless in this strict atmosphere.

For Clarice It Is Terrible Because with This He Takes Away All the Popular Songs and the Moonlights and Still Night Hushes and the Movies with Star-eyed Girls and Simpering Males

They were going to have so much fun in the summer.
But winter has come to the edges of his regard.
Not the lace-ice, but the bleak, the bleak steep sorrow.
Not the shy snow, not the impermanent icicles but the hard
The cruel pack and snarl of the unloved cold.

There is nowhere for her to go.
There is no tenderness on whom she may frankly cry.
There is no way to unlatch her face
And show the gray shudder
Of this hurt hour
And the desert death of tomorrow.

Jack

is not spendthrift of faith.
He has a skinny eye.
He spends a wariness of faith.
He puts his other by.

And comes it up his faith bought true,
He spends a little more.
And comes it up his faith bought false,
It's long gone from the store.

A Penitent Considers Another Coming of Mary

FOR REVEREND THEODORE RICHARDSON

If Mary came would Mary
Forgive, as Mothers may,
And sad and second Saviour
Furnish us today?

She would not shake her head and leave
This military air,
But ratify a modern hay,
And put her Baby there.

Mary would not punish men —
If Mary came again.

Bronzeville Woman in a Red Hat

HIRES OUT TO
MRS. MILES

I

They had never had one in the house before.
        The strangeness of it all. Like unleashing
A lion, really. Poised
To pounce. A puma. A panther. A black
Bear.
There it stood in the door,
Under a red hat that was rash, but refreshing —
In a tasteless way, of course — across the dull dare,
The semi-assault of that extraordinary blackness.
The slackness
Of that light pink mouth told little. The eyes told of heavy
  care. . . .
But that was neither here nor there,
And nothing to a wage-paying mistress as should
Be getting her due whether life had been good
For her slave, or bad.

There it stood
In the door. They had never had
One in the house before.

But the Irishwoman had left!
A message had come.
Something about a murder at home.
A daughter's husband — "berserk," that was the phrase:
The dear man had "gone berserk"
And short work —
With a hammer — had been made
Of this daughter and her nights and days.
The Irishwoman (underpaid,
Mrs. Miles remembered with smiles),
Who was a perfect jewel, a red-faced trump,
A good old sort, a baker
Of rum cake, a maker
Of Mustard, would never return.
Mrs. Miles had begged the bewitched woman
To finish, at least, the biscuit blending,
To tarry till the curry was done,
To show some concern
For the burning soup, to attend to the tending
Of the tossed salad. "Inhuman,"
Patsy Houlihan had called Mrs. Miles.
"Inhuman." And "a fool."
And "a cool
One."

The Alert Agency had leafed through its files —
On short notice could offer
Only this dusky duffer
That now made its way to her kitchen and sat on her kitchen stool.

II

Her creamy child kissed by the black maid! square on the mouth!
World yelled, world writhed, world turned to light and rolled
Into her kitchen, nearly knocked her down.

Quotations, of course, from baby books were great
Ready armor; (but her animal distress
Wore, too and under, a subtler metal dress,
Inheritance of approximately hate).
Say baby shrieked to see his finger bleed,
Wished human humoring — there was a kind
Of unintimate love, a love more of the mind
To order the nebulousness of that need.
— This was the way to put it, this the relief.
This sprayed a honey upon marvelous grime.
This told it possible to postpone the reef.
Fashioned a huggable darling out of crime.
Made monster personable in personal sight
By cracking mirrors down the personal night.

Disgust crawled through her as she chased the theme.
She, quite supposing purity despoiled,
Committed to sourness, disordered, soiled,
Went in to pry the ordure from the cream.
Cooing, "Come." (Come out of the cannibal wilderness,
Dirt, dark, into the sun and bloomful air.
Return to freshness of your right world, wear
Sweetness again. Be done with beast, duress.)

Child with continuing cling issued his No in final fire,
Kissed back the colored maid,
Not wise enough to freeze or be afraid.
Conscious of kindness, easy creature bond.
Love had been handy and rapid to respond.

Heat at the hairline, heat between the bowels,
Examining seeming coarse unnatural scene,
She saw all things except herself serene:
Child, big black woman, pretty kitchen towels.

The Contemplation of Suicide: The Temptation of Timothy

One poises, poses, at track, or range, or river,
Saying, What is the fact of my life, to what do I tend? —
And is it assured and sweet that I have come, after mazes and robins, after the foodless swallowings and snatchings at fog, to this foppish end?
(Knowing that downtown the sluggish shrug their shoulders, slink, talk.)

Then, though one can think of no fact, no path, no ground,
Some little thing, remarkless and daily, relates
Its common cliché. One lunges or lags on, prates. —
Too selfish to be nothing while beams break, surf's epileptic, chicken reeks or squalls.

On the Occasion of the Open-air Formation of the Olde Tymers' Walking and Nature Club

We shall go playing in the woods again!
The flowers and fruits and nuts and sun have waited.
And when we come, we merry girls and men,
They will unlock themselves, and be elated.

And we shall walk among them, working well
At this delicious business of being gay.
And we shall push our laughter like a bell,
Trying to make it ring in the old way.

But if our romp is rusty, if we fumble,
If we fall down, and if our festival
Of molded mirth should crack, or even crumble,
Have mercy, flowers! sun, forgive us all.

Bessie of Bronzeville Visits Mary and Norman at a Beach-house in New Buffalo

You said, "Now take your shoes off," while what played
Was not the back-town boogie but a green
Wet music stuff, above the wide and clean
Sand, and my hand laughed.
Toes urged the slab to amber foam.

And I was hurt by cider in the air.
And what the lake-wash did was dizzying.
I thought of England, as I watched you bring
The speckled pebbles,
The smooth quartz; I thought of Italy.

Italy and England come.
A sea sits up and starts to sing to me.

Naomi

Too foraging to blue-print or deploy! —
To lift her brother;
Or tell dull mother
That is not it among the dishes and brooms,
It is damper
Than what you will wipe out of sills and down from the
  mouldings of rooms
And dump from the dirty-clothes hamper;

Or say "Do not bother
To hug your cheese and furniture"
To her small father;

Or to register at all the hope of her hunt or say what
It was not.

(It was, by diligent caring,
To find out what life was for.

For certainly what it was not for was forbearing.)

Callie Ford

It's a day for running out of town
With a man whose eyes are brown.

We'll go where trees leap up out of hills
And flowers are not planned.
We'll be happy all our day.
First, he must press my hand,
In the afternoon discover my waist,
At night my mouth, and ask for the taste.
And he must call me "very sweet."
And I must call him "clever."

We'll come back
Together at dawn
And hate each other forever.

The Ballad of Rudolph Reed

Rudolph Reed was oaken.
His wife was oaken too.
And his two good girls and his good little man
Oakened as they grew.

"I am not hungry for berries.
I am not hungry for bread.
But hungry hungry for a house
Where at night a man in bed

"May never hear the plaster
Stir as if in pain.
May never hear the roaches
Falling like fat rain.

"Where never wife and children need
Go blinking through the gloom.
Where every room of many rooms
Will be full of room.

"Oh my home may have its east or west
Or north or south behind it.
All I know is I shall know it,
And fight for it when I find it."

It was in a street of bitter white
That he made his application.
For Rudolph Reed was oakener
Than others in the nation.

The agent's steep and steady stare
Corroded to a grin.
Why, you black old, tough old hell of a man,
Move your family in!

Nary a grin grinned Rudolph Reed,
Nary a curse cursed he,
But moved in his House. With his dark little wife,
And his dark little children three.

A neighbor would *look*, with a yawning eye
That squeezed into a slit.
But the Rudolph Reeds and the children three
Were too joyous to notice it.

For were they not firm in a home of their own
With windows everywhere
And a beautiful banistered stair
And a front yard for flowers and a back yard for grass?

The first night, a rock, big as two fists.
The second, a rock big as three.
But nary a curse cursed Rudolph Reed.
(Though oaken as man could be.)

The third night, a silvery ring of glass.
Patience ached to endure.
But he looked, and lo! small Mabel's blood
Was staining her gaze so pure.

Then up did rise our Rudolph Reed
And pressed the hand of his wife,
And went to the door with a thirty-four
And a beastly butcher knife.

He ran like a mad thing into the night.
And the words in his mouth were stinking.
By the time he had hurt his first white man
He was no longer thinking.

By the time he had hurt his fourth white man
Rudolph Reed was dead.
His neighbors gathered and kicked his corpse.
"Nigger —" his neighbors said.

Small Mabel whimpered all night long,
For calling herself the cause.
Her oak-eyed mother did no thing
But change the bloody gauze.

Priscilla Assails the Sepulchre of Love

I can't unlock my eyes because
My body will come through
And cut her every clothing off
And drive herself to you

Who want no sort of gift outright
Nor one that simpers back
Nor one that sorrows off, but none,
And laugh above your lack.

I keep my keys away that she
May never have to find
The enameled winter of your heart,
The pastels of your mind.

Leftist Orator in Washington Park Pleasantly Punishes the Gropers

Poor Pale-eyed, thrice-gulping Amazed.
It is white and rushed here, this is a crazy snow.
I am afraid the wind will not falter at any time in the night.
I know you are frightened and I know
You know not where to go.

I foretell the heat and yawn of eye and the drop of the mouth and the screech,
The foolish, unhappy screech hanging high on the air.
Because you had no dream or belief or reach.
Because you could only beseech.

Because you were nothing, saw nothing, did nothing at all.
Because there will be No Thing for which you fall.

The Artists' and Models' Ball

(FOR FRANK SHEPHERD)

Wonders do not confuse. We call them that
And close the matter there. But common things
Surprise us. They accept the names we give
With calm, and keep them. Easy-breathing then
We brave our next small business. Well, behind
Our backs they alter. How were we to know.

The Egg Boiler

Being you, you cut your poetry from wood.
The boiling of an egg is heavy art.
You come upon it as an artist should,
With rich-eyed passion, and with straining heart.
We fools, we cut our poems out of air,
Night color, wind soprano, and such stuff.
And sometimes weightlessness is much to bear.
You mock it, though, you name it Not Enough.
The egg, spooned gently to the avid pan,
And left the strict three minutes, or the four,
Is your Enough and art for any man.
We fools give courteous ear — then cut some more,
Shaping a gorgeous Nothingness from cloud.
You watch us, eat your egg, and laugh aloud.

In Emanuel's Nightmare: Another Coming of Christ

(SPEAKS, AMONG SPIRIT QUESTIONERS, OF MARVELOUS SPIRIT AFFAIRS)

There had been quiet all that afternoon.
Just such a quiet afternoon as any,
Though with a brighter and a freer air.
The sleepy sun sat on us, and those clouds
Dragged dreamily. Well, it was interesting —
How silence could give place to such a noise.
But now — is noise the word? Is that exact?
I think not.

I'll try to name it. Naming is my line.
I won the Great War-Naming Contest. Ah,
I put it over on them all. I beat
Them all. I wear an honor on my name —

Sound wasn't in it. Though it was loud enough.
I'd say it was a heat.

But it took us. Did with us as it would.
Wound us in balls, unraveled, wound again.
And women screamed "The Judgment Day has come."
And little children gathered up the cry.
It was then that they knocked each other down
To get to — Where? But they were used to Doors.
Thought they had but to beat their Fellow Man
To get to and get out of one again.

It wasn't Judgment Day. (For we are here.)
And presently the people knew, and sighed.
Out of that heaven a most beautiful Man
Came down. But now is coming quite the word?
It wasn't coming. I'd say it was — a Birth.
The man was born out of the heaven, in truth.
Yet no parturient creature ever knew
That naturalness, that hurtlessness, that ease.

How He was tall and strong!
How He was cold-browed! How He mildly smiled!
How the voice played on the heavy hope of the air
And loved our hearts out!
Why, it was such a voice as gave me eyes
To see my Fellow Man of all the world,
There with me, listening.

He had come down, He said, to clean the earth
Of the dirtiness of war.

Now tell of why His power failed Him there?
His power did not fail. It was that, simply,
He found how much the people wanted war.
How much it was their creed, and their good joy.
And what they lived for. He had not the heart
To take away their chief sweet delectation.

We tear — as a decent gesture, a tact — we tear
Laxly again at our lax, our tired hair.

The people wanted war. War's in their hearts.
    (In me, in your snag-toothed fool
Who won the Great War-Naming Contest and
All the years since has bragged how he did Beat
His Fellow Man.) It is the human aim.
Without, there would be no hate. No Diplomats.
And households would be fresh and frictionless.

God's Son went home. Among us it is whispered
He cried the tears of men.

Feeling, in fact,
We have no need of peace.

Set in Scotch Roman
Format by Cy Axelrad
Manufactured by The Haddon Craftsmen, Inc.
Published by HARPER & BROTHERS, *New York*

CPSIA information can be obtained
at www.ICGtesting.com
Printed in the USA
BVHW061537120720
583443BV00005B/729

9 781258 274481